Engaging God's Word

Job

Engage Bible Studies

Tools That Transform

Engage Bible Studies

an imprint of

 COMMUNITY BIBLE STUDY

Engaging God's Word: Job
Copyright © 2012 by Community Bible Study. All rights reserved.
ISBN 978-1-62194-013-5

Published by Community Bible Study
790 Stout Road
Colorado Springs, CO
1-800-826-4181
www.communitybiblestudy.org

Printed in the United States of America.

Contents

Introduction

Welcome to the life-changing adventure of engaging with God's Word! Whether this is the first time you've opened a Bible or you've studied the Scriptures all your life, good things are in store for you. Studying the Bible is unlike any other kind of study you have ever done. That's because the Word of God is *"living and active"* (Hebrews 4:12) and transcends time and cultures. The earth and heavens as we know them will one day pass away, but God's Word never will (Mark 13:31). It's as relevant to your life today as it was to the people who wrote it down centuries ago. And the fact that God's Word is living and active means that reading God's Word is always meant to be a personal experience. God's Word is not just dead words on a page—it is page after page of living, powerful words—so get ready, because the time you spend studying the Bible in this *Engaging God's Word* course will be life-transforming!

Why Study the Bible?

Some Christians read the Bible because they know they're supposed to. It's a good thing to do, and God expects it. And all that's true! However, there are many additional reasons to study God's Word. Here are just some of them.

We get to know God through His Word. Our God is a relational God who knows us and wants us to know Him. The Scriptures, which He authored, reveal much about Him: how He thinks and feels, what His purposes are, what He thinks about us, how He views the world He made, what He has planned for the future. The Bible shows us God's many attributes—His kindness, goodness, justice, love, faithfulness, mercy, compassion, creativity, redemption, sovereignty, and so on. As we get to know Him through His Word, we come to love and trust Him.

God speaks to us through His Word. One of the primary ways God speaks to us is through His written Word. Don't be surprised if, as you read the Bible, certain parts nearly jump off the page at you, almost as if they'd been written with you in mind. God is the Author of this incredible book, so that's not just possible, it's likely! Whether it is to find comfort, warning, correction, teaching, or guidance, always approach God's Word with your spiritual ears open (Isaiah 55:3) because God, your loving heavenly Father, has things He wants to say to you.

God's Word brings life. Just about everyone wants to learn the secret to "the good life." And the good news is, that secret is found in God's Word. Don't think of the Bible as a bunch of rules. Viewing it with that mindset is a distortion. God gave us His Word because as our Creator and the Creator of the universe, He alone knows how life was meant to work. He knows that love makes us happier than hate, that generosity brings more joy than greed, and that integrity allows us to rest more peacefully at night than deception does. God's ways are not always "easiest" but they are the way to life. As the Psalmist says, *"If Your law had not been my delight, I would have perished in my affliction. I will never forget Your precepts, for by them You have given me life"* (Psalm 119:92-93).

God's Word offers stability in an unstable world. Truth is an ever-changing negotiable for many people in our culture today. But building your life on constantly changing "truth" is like building your house on shifting sand. God's Word, like God Himself, never changes. What He says was true yesterday, is true today, and will still be true a billion years from now. Jesus said, *"Everyone then who hears these words of Mine and does them will be like a wise man who built his house on the rock"* (Matthew 7:24).

God's Word helps us to pray effectively. When we read God's Word and get to know what He is really like, we understand better how to pray. God answers prayers that are according to His will. We discover His will by reading the Bible. First John 5:14-15 tells us that *"this is the confidence that we have toward Him, that if we ask anything according to His will He hears us. And if we know that He hears us in whatever we ask, we know that we have the requests that we have asked of Him."*

How to Get the Most
out of *Engaging God's Word*

Each *Engaging God's Word* study contains key elements that have been carefully designed to help you get the most out of your time in God's Word. Slightly modified for your study-at-home success, this approach is very similar to the tried-and-proven Bible study method that Community Bible Study has used with thousands of men, women, and children across the United States and around the world for nearly 40 years. There are some basic things you can expect to find in each course in this series.

* Lesson 1 provides an overview of the Bible book (or books) you will study and questions to help you focus, anticipate, and pray about what you will be learning.

* Every lesson contains questions to answer on your own, commentary that reviews and clarifies the passage, and three special sections called "Apply what you have learned," "Think about" and "Personalize this lesson."

* Some lessons contain memory verse suggestions.

Whether you plan to use *Engaging God's Word* on your own or with a group, here are some suggestions that will help you enjoy and receive the most benefit from your study.

Spread out each lesson over several days. Your *Engaging God's Word* lessons were designed to take a week to complete. Spreading out your study rather than doing it all at once allows time for the things God is teaching you to sink in and for you to practice applying them.

Pray each time you read God's Word. The Bible is a book unlike any other because God Himself inspired it. The same Spirit who inspired the human authors who wrote it will help you to understand and apply it if you ask Him to. So make it a practice to ask Him to make His Word come alive to you every time you read it.

Read the whole passage covered in the lesson. Before plunging into the questions, take time to read the specific chapter or verses that will be covered in that lesson. Doing this will give you important context for the whole lesson. Reading the Bible in context is an important principle in interpreting it accurately.

Begin learning the memory verse. Learning Scripture by heart requires discipline, but the rewards far outweigh the effort. Memorizing a verse allows you to recall it whenever you need it—for personal encouragement and direction, or to share with someone else. Consider writing the verse on a sticky note or index card that you can post where you will see it often or carry with you to review during the day. Reading and re-reading the verse often—out loud when possible—is a simple way to commit it to memory.

Re-read the passage for each section of questions. Each lesson is divided into sections so that you study one small part of Scripture at a time. Before attempting to answer the questions, review the verses that the questions will cover.

Answer the questions without consulting the Commentary or other reference materials. There is great joy in having the Holy Spirit teach you God's Word on your own, without the help of outside resources. Don't cheat yourself of the delight of discovery by reading the Commentary prematurely. Wait until after you've completed the lesson.

Repeat the process for all the question sections.

Prayerfully consider the "Apply what you have learned," marked with the 📌 push pin symbol. The vision of Community Bible Study is not to just gain knowledge about the Bible, but to be transformed by it. For this reason, each set of questions closes with a section that encourages you to apply what you are learning. Usually this section involves action—something for you to do. As you practice these suggestions, your life will change.

Read the Commentary. *Engaging God's Word* commentaries are written by theologians whose goal is to help you understand the context of what you are studying as it relates to the rest of Scripture, God's character, and what the passage means for your life. Of necessity, the commentaries include the author's interpretations. While interesting and helpful, keep in mind that the Commentary is simply one person's understanding of what these passages mean. Other godly men and women have views that are also worth considering.

Pause to contemplate each "Think about" section, marked with the notepad symbol. These features, embedded in the Commentary, offer a place to pause and consider some of the principles being brought out by the text. They provide excellent ideas to journal about or to discuss with other believers, especially those doing the study with you.

Jot down insights or prayer points from the "Personalize this lesson" marked with the ☑ check box symbol. While the "Apply what you have learned" section focuses on doing, the "Personalize this lesson" section focuses on becoming. Spiritual transformation is not just about doing right things and refraining from doing wrong things—it is about changing from the inside out. To be transformed means letting God change our hearts so that our attitudes, emotions, desires, reactions, and goals are increasingly like Jesus'. Often this section will discuss something that you cannot do in your own strength—so your response will usually be something to pray about. Remember that becoming more Christ-like is not just a matter of trying harder—it requires God's empowerment.

The Beginning of Job's Trials
Job 1:1-5

Job is a book of conversations. It opens with a conversation in heaven between God and Satan. God uses Job as an example of a righteous and faithful man. Then God gives Satan permission to test Job and see just how steadfast he is. The story then shifts to earth, where dreadful calamities come Job's way. He loses his children, his wealth, his possessions and even his health—without ever knowing why any of this is happening.

The majority of the book takes the form of poetic, conversational rounds between Job and four of his friends. Job reacts to his intense suffering as a normal human would. He questions, laments, grieves, and wishes he had never been born. He insists he did nothing wrong, and wonders why God is doing this to him. He goes further, questioning God and asking why God would cause an innocent man to suffer. His friends attempt to pinpoint what Job has done wrong and to explain what God is up to. Finally, after many chapters, God speaks … and that changes everything!

Some of the themes you'll encounter in the book of Job include:

❖ The causes of suffering and the questions we ask when we do

❖ Time-worn (and unhelpful) views of why God allows people to suffer

❖ How we respond to God during times of suffering

❖ God's sovereignty

❖ Our appropriate response upon experiencing God as He truly is

1. During his time of deep suffering, Job asks God, "Why?" Can
    you relate to asking God a question such as this? What was the
    experience like for you?

    _____

    _____

    _____

    _____

2. When you ask God a "why" question, what answer do you hope
    to receive?

    _____

    _____

3. How have times of suffering affected your ability to relate with
    God?

    _____

    _____

4. What has helped you endure through these times?

    _____

    _____

    _____

*If you are doing this study with a group, listen to one another's answers to the
questions above. Avoid any urges to offer advice or compare your experiences.
Instead, take time to pray for one another, asking God to use the study of Job
to deepen your experiences of God's love and sovereignty, even in hard times.
If you are doing this study alone, talk with God about what you hope to
receive from Him over the next six weeks of this study.*

Lesson 1 Commentary

The Beginning of Job's Trials
Job 1:1-5

The book of Job tells of one man's struggle to comprehend how God's goodness relates to his suffering. God affirms that Job is especially righteous. Still, God permits him to suffer the loss of everything dear to him. The book pulls back the curtain of heaven and permits the reader to learn about matters that were concealed from Job. Had he known that his sufferings were significant, he might have found them easier to bear. Job's ignorance helps to aggravate his suffering, but it also makes the book realistic. We can understand more about our own troubles from Job's experience. We can learn what it looks like to question God yet still surrender to Him.

Date

Job lives in the land of Uz. Although its exact location is unknown, Uz was certainly outside the boundaries of Israel—probably in northern Arabia, in the region of Edom (see Lamentations 4:21). No time period is indicated in the book, but it is likely that the events are some of the earliest in the Bible. The book contains no reference to the Ten Commandments, Israel, or the Hebrew covenants. Job acts as a priest on behalf of his own family. The most common name for God in the book is *Shaddai (Almighty)* rather than *Yahweh (Lord)*, the name by which God revealed Himself to Israel. For these and other reasons, it is best to regard the book of Job as set in the period before the giving of the Mosaic Law, which took place about 1440 BC. In fact, the book exhibits many points of contact with the time of Abraham, Isaac, and Jacob.

When was the book composed? Someone might have written of these events much later. However, much of Job is direct quotation, leading to the premise that whoever wrote the book must either have been an eyewitness of these conversations or had a reliable record of them. The writing of Job must have either been undertaken when the events happened or the raw materials—the conversations—must have gained written form at that time.

Authorship

No author is mentioned in the book itself. As a result, many names have been proposed as the writer, including Job himself, Moses, Elihu (a man who appears in the book), and Solomon. Some have thought that Job could not be the author, because the book is written in the third person. However, many biblical authors (including Moses) wrote of themselves in the third person.

Literary Characteristics

Most of Job is poetry, but the opening two chapters and the closing section are prose. Hebrew poetry generally consists of paired lines that rhyme. The rhyming, however, is not that of sounds, but of thoughts. Therefore, you will see repeated concepts. For example, Job complains, *"The eye of him who sees me will behold me no more; while your eyes are on me, I shall be gone"* (Job 7:8). Repetition gives force and power to the words.

It must be remembered that a large portion of the book (particularly chapters 4–26) contains *bad advice.* Job's three friends spoke freely and often incorrectly (see 42:7). The Bible contains such material because it is important to know how to identify and respond to such false assertions.

Purpose

The book of Job is aimed at helping readers see how God's ways are far above our own. Job is not primarily a book about suffering; it is a book about the sovereignty of God and one's proper relationship to Him. Job teaches that there are limits to our curiosity about why God allows some suffering to occur. Believers may suffer undeservedly, yet they must be willing to trust God and acknowledge that He knows best.

The book outlines in very clear terms the relationship between God and the pain that sometimes enter our lives. God (whose intentions are ever good) permits Satan (whose intentions are persistently hostile) to inflict damage on a righteous person. The book of Job shows the outcome of Satan's schemes. Throughout Scripture, a struggle between unseen beings is revealed. The world we inhabit is complex, made more so by the fact that unseen beings (angels) as well as visible creatures (mankind) are in rebellion against God.

Lurking in the background of this book, although unstated, is the problem of interpreting human suffering. When human beings—who have done nothing that would ordinarily merit divine discipline—suffer, two questions often torment us: Is God treating us unjustly? Or are we somehow just getting what we deserve? In Job's case, neither was true.

Who Is Job?

This remarkable book opens with a description of Job, a man who is *"blameless and upright"* (1:1). The author does not suggest that Job is sinless, but that he is a person of sterling character and spiritual maturity who has sustained a consistent, healthy relationship with God. Job also *"feared God and turned away from evil."* The term *fear* does not mean the fear that produces avoidance, but the caution that would rather do anything than offend.

Job possesses great wealth and a large family, about whose spiritual welfare he is intensely concerned. Although it is mentioned only in passing here, Job is a highly respected member of the community: *"When I went out to the gate of the city, when I prepared my seat in the square, the young men saw me and withdrew, and the aged rose and stood; the princes refrained from talking. ... When the ear heard, it called me blessed, and when the eye saw, it approved"* (29:7-11).

Job is mentioned three other times in the Bible outside the book of Job. Twice in Ezekiel, God names him alongside Daniel and Noah as a righteous person (Ezekiel 14:14, 20). In the New Testament, the epistle of James exhorts readers to imitate Job's endurance: *"You have heard of the steadfastness of Job, and you have seen the purpose of the Lord, how the Lord is compassionate and merciful"* (James 5:11).

Personalize this lesson.

☑ Sudden calamity occurs when we are victimized by other people, have an accident or medical emergency, or encounter a natural disaster. Job is an example of someone prepared for crisis—he walked closely and openly with God. When chaos erupts around us and familiar structures disappear (as when a tornado or wildfire wipes out a town), we should be so in tune to the Father that we can hear His voice and respond to His guidance. When the things we depend on are destroyed, we can turn to God and ask Him to provide whatever we need. Resting in Him will not erase the sorrow, pain, or fear that we feel, but it will keep us from becoming overwhelmed.

Walking daily with Jesus is your best "security blanket." If you haven't already, begin now to nurture that close relationship by letting the Lord into every area of your life. Talk with Him about every aspect of your normal life; turn to Him in big matters and small. Come to Him freely to experience His care, delight, fellowship, and parenting. Ask Him to reveal who He is to you and to help you know Him truly. Also deal with the hidden sins; confess them and accept the gracious cleansing that Jesus provided through His death on the cross. *"If we walk in the light, as He is in the light, we have fellowship with one another, and the blood of Jesus His Son cleanses us from all sin"* (1 John 1:7). Job's life was *"blameless"* before the Lord (Job 1:7) and he enjoyed *"the friendship of God"* upon his tent (29:4). We should be so familiar with God's voice that we respond to Him quickly and gladly, as we would a dear Friend and caring Father. The best preparation for disaster is a close walk with God.

The Trials and Testings of Job
Job 1:6-2:10

Memorize God's Word: Job 1:21.

❖ Job 1:1-12—The Beginning of Job's Trials

1. Read Job 1:1-5. What do these verses reveal about Job's faith, his family, and his fortune?

   _____

   _____

   _____

2. What does Job 1:6-12 tell us about
   a. God? _____

   _____

   _____

   b. Satan? _____

   _____

   _____

3. The Hebrew word translated *Satan* literally means the *Accuser*. In 1:6-12, what accusations does Satan make?

   _____

   _____

   _____

   _____

4. How does God respond?

    _____

    _____

5. Why might Satan want to challenge Job's motive for worshiping God?

    _____

    _____

❖ Job 1:13-22—Job Under Attack

6. In Job 1:13-22, what assaults does Satan inflict on Job?

    _____

    _____

    _____

7. What do these attacks reveal about Satan's power?

    _____

    _____

8. What do they reveal about God?

    _____

    _____

9. How does Job's response to these assaults prove God right and Satan wrong?

    _____

    _____

    _____

❖ Job 2:1-8—Another Assault on a Righteous Man

10. In Job 2, Satan again appears in God's throne room. When God questions him, what does Satan say he has been doing?

    _____

    _____

11. According to the following Scriptures, what are Satan's tactics and objectives?

   a. John 8:44 _____

   _____

   _____

   b. 2 Corinthians 4:4_____

   _____

   _____

   c. 1 Peter 5:8_____

   _____

   _____

12. What is Satan's primary objective in Job's case, and how does he plan to accomplish it?

   _____

   _____

   _____

13. What does the fact that God set limits on Satan (Job 1:12, 2:6) say about Satan's power?

   _____

   _____

   _____

❖ Job 2:9-10—Spousal Advice

14. Satan directed his attacks against Job, but other people were affected, too—especially Job's wife. Consider the losses Mrs. Job suffered. Why might she tell Job to *"curse God and die"*?

   _____

   _____

   _____

   _____

15. How does Job respond?

_____

_____

_____

16. Have you ever felt like Job's wife in the face of great suffering—
    or known someone who has? What can this conversation
    between Job and his wife show us as we relate with friends or
    loved ones who are suffering?

_____

_____

_____

_____

_____

_____

Apply what you have learned. Waves of
tragedy have overwhelmed Job, yet the first words
out of his mouth are, *"Naked I came from my mother's
womb, and naked shall I return. The Lord gave, and the Lord
has taken away; blessed be the name of the Lord"* (1:21).
These are amazing words, requiring tremendous humility,
wisdom, and respect for God. Job somehow understands
that although God is permitting the terrible things that are
happening, He does not take delight in them. *"Job did not
sin or charge God with wrong"* (1:22). Job's relationship with
God during normal days had prepared him to honor God
even during difficult trials. It would be wise for us, also, to
deepen our relationships with God when we aren't in times
of suffering so that we are able to relate well with God and
honor Him when our souls are in distress.

The Trials and Testings of Job
Job 1:6-2:10

God displays His delight in Job by showering blessings on him. It is on those blessings that the plot of the book now turns. Satan will contend that Job's uprightness is merely a means to an end.

First Dialogue Between God and Satan

Many people in the modern world—even Christians—regard Satan as a fantasy or a mere influence. The Bible does not support these views. Jesus held an extended conversation with the tempter in the wilderness (Luke 4:1-12). Jesus didn't talk with an *influence,* nor is God indulging in an imaginary conversation here in Job 1. Satan is all too real. He is loose in the world and continues to attack Christians (1 Peter 5:8; Revelation 2:10). However, he is a creature and has limits. He is not God's equal, though opposite, counterpart (this idea is *dualism,* which the Bible does not teach). There is only one Supreme Being: God, and He is wholly righteous. God causes no evil and no harm; however, He does permit it for His own sufficient reasons. Satan can do no more damage to a believer than God permits.

For reasons never explained, God proposes that Satan consider Job. Satan asserts that Job does not truly love God; he merely uses Him. The Almighty is the source of Job's vast wealth. If those possessions were removed, Job would renounce God and curse Him openly. God is indeed responsible for Job's prosperity, but Satan is wrong about Job's motives. Mixing truth and error in this way is characteristic of satanic strategy.

Think about Satan's part in life's troubles. Satan's influence is often so subtle that we may not recognize it. He will whisper lies to us: *"There is no truth in him. When he lies, he speaks out of his own character, for he is a liar and the father of lies"* (John 8:44). He will try to pin the blame for every problem on God. He will tell us that God doesn't care about us, that He has forgotten about us, or that He has turned His back on us. But we don't have to fall for these whispers. Though Satan would like to twist our thinking so we accuse God or turn away from Him, we can instead run to God. *"The Lord is good, a stronghold in the day of trouble; He knows those who take refuge in Him"* (Nahum 1:7).

The scene shifts from heaven to earth, where Satan uses hostile neighbors to play out his evil designs. The Sabeans raid Job's vast herds of oxen and donkeys and kill Job's servants. While a first messenger delivers this report, another arrives with more bad news: *"The fire of God fell from heaven and burned up the sheep and the servants and consumed them"* (Job 1:16). *"The fire of God"* could describe a supernatural act, or this phrase could be a figure of speech describing lightning bolts. Then a third messenger arrives to report the loss of Job's camels and their herdsmen. By this time, Job's wealth lies in ruins—but worse is yet to come. A fourth messenger brings news that a strong wind has collapsed the house where Job's children were feasting, killing them all.

Job reacts by tearing his robe and shaving his head, signs of great mourning (Genesis 37:34; Micah 1:16). Then, amazingly, he falls to the ground in worship. He acknowledges God's right to take away all he had. After all, God had given it to him in the first place. God is the same whether prosperity or ruin is allowed into our lives. He deserves the same worship under good or ill circumstances (Habakkuk 3:17-18).

Second Dialogue Between God and Satan

Sometime after Job's initial devastation, Satan again reports to the Lord. God asks, *"From where have you come?"* God is not trying to gain information; He is exposing Satan's work. Satan now argues that self-preservation is a person's only significant motive: *"All that a man has he will give for his life."* Satan predicts that Job's integrity is about to end: *"Stretch out Your hand and touch his bone and his flesh, and he will curse You to Your face"* (2:5).

God again places Job in Satan's hands, but restricts the devastation: *"Spare his life."* Armed with divine permission, Satan jumps into the task with enthusiasm; *"Satan went out from the presence of the Lord and struck Job with loathsome sores from the sole of his foot to the crown of his head"* (2:7). Job's affliction, whatever it is, has such severe physical effects that his friends fail to recognize him. Surrounded by loss and ruin, Job's wife suggests he end it all and curse God. Surely, she reasons, God would not permit a human to curse Him; Job would die for his impertinence, but at least he would be out of his misery.

Think about Job's response to his wife: *"Shall we receive good from God, and shall we not receive evil?"* (2:10). This question is key to the book of Job. Job trusted God through adversities as well as blessings. If we believe God is sovereign, then we must also face the reality that hardships may be within His will for us. The apostle Paul says: *"I know how to be brought low, and I know how to abound. In any and every circumstance, I have learned the secret of facing plenty and hunger, abundance and need. I can do all things through Him who strengthens me"* (Philippians 4:12-13). We can't avoid trouble, but we can draw close to God and lean on His strength during it.

Job's worldview is clear. The good things in the world reflect God's gracious kindness. Is it reasonable that we should turn away from God if He also allows calamity to come our way? God's assessment of Job's response to his wife's advice is clear: *"In all this Job did not sin with his lips"* (2:10).

Personalize this lesson.

Life is characterized by change, and change often means loss. Although everything we have is a gift from God, we tend to expect Him always to bless us and never to take back any of His gifts. Our comfortable lifestyles, our good health, our loving relationships, our satisfying careers and pursuits—are all vulnerable to change. In Psalm 42, the psalmist looks past the painful time he is experiencing and twice reminds himself, *"Why are you cast down, O my soul, and why are you in turmoil within me? Hope in God; for I shall again praise Him, my salvation and my God"* (Psalm 42:5-6, 11). We can trust God to renew His blessings and restore our lost peace and comfort sometime in the future. While God may not restore exactly what we have lost, He can bring new sources of joy to us.

Lesson 3
Bad Advice and Unfair Accusations
Job 2:11–26:6

Memorize God's Word: Job 23:10b.

❖ Job 2:11–3:26—The Friends of a Suffering Man

1. Who are Job's three friends, and why do they come (2:11)?

2. How can their initial response guide us when we seek to comfort a suffering friend?

3. How would you summarize Job's lament in 3:1-4, 20-26?

❖ Job 4–7—Eliphaz: Round I

4. Read Job 4:1-9; 5:17-18. According to Eliphaz, why do people suffer?

5. How would you describe Job's state of mind as he responds to Eliphaz (6:1-13)?

_____

_____

_____

6. What does Job say about his friends in 6:14-17, 21-26?

_____

_____

_____

7. What appeal does Job make to God at this time (7:11-21)?

_____

_____

❖ Job 8–14—Bildad and Zophar: Round I

8. What approach does Bildad take as he attempts to explain Job's suffering (8:1-6)?

_____

_____

9. What attribute of God does Bildad emphasize?

_____

_____

10. What attributes of God are missing from Bildad's view of Him? (See Lamentations 3:22-23; 1 Timothy 1:13-16.)

_____

_____

11. What does Job believe it would take for him to have a fair hearing before God (9:32-34)?

_____

_____

12. Job talks of an *"arbiter"* in 9:33. To whom does this passage prophetically refer? (See 1 Timothy 2:5; 1 John 2:1.)

_____

_____

13. When Zophar speaks up, what points does he make (Job 11:1-6; Job 11:13-20)?

_____

_____

14. How does Job answer Zophar's accusations (12:1-4; 13:1-5)?

_____

_____

_____

15. Because we have God's full written revelation, the Bible, we know more than Job did about what happens after death. What question concerning life after death does Job raise in 14:14?

_____

_____

16. What answer could you give a friend who asked that question today (John 14:1-3; Hebrews 9:27-28)?

_____

_____

❖ Job 15–21—Job and His Friends: Round II

17. What attack does Eliphaz open with in Round II (15:1-6)?

_____

_____

18. Although Job feels that God is using him for target practice (16:6-14), where does he continue to look for help (16:19-21)?

_____

_____

19. Why does Job feel he deserves pity from his friends instead of condemnation (19:19-22)?

_____

_____

20. What name does Job use for God in 19:25-27?

_____

21. What hope does Job express in this passage? What would it look like for you to have that hope?

_____

_____

❖ Job 22–26—Job and His Friends: Round III

22. Even though Job continues to express confidence in his ultimate vindication (23:10-12), what complaints does he voice against God in 23:1-5?

_____

_____

23. Job asks an insightful question in his brief response to Bildad (26:4). How would you answer it? (See John 8:44.)

_____

_____

Apply what you have learned. How easy it is to falsely accuse people or doubt their motives! *"Judge not, and you will not be judged; condemn not, and you will not be condemned; forgive, and you will be forgiven"* (Luke 6:37). We don't want to be like Job's friends, whose judgmental attitudes just heaped more pain on an already-hurting Job. What is one way you could avoid doing this when you are talking with a hurting friend? How could you display God's heart toward your friend?

Bad Advice and Unfair Accusations
Job 2:11-26:6

The center section of Job follows a pattern: Job's three friends speak to him in turn, and Job responds to their criticism. There are three cycles of debate. All three friends speak from the same overriding theological viewpoint: People get what they deserve. Job's sufferings are the consequence of his hidden sin; he should acknowledge it and repent so God can again bless him. Job denies any sin and insists he would be vindicated if he could somehow gain a hearing before an impartial judge. Job also claims God has treated him unfairly.

The Sympathetic Silence of Job's Friends

Job's three friends apparently love him, for they are stricken when they see him. At first, the friends do exactly the right thing; they enter into Job's pain and silently share it with him for seven days. People in extreme pain are rarely interested in advice; they want to know if anyone can understand what they are going through. Compassion waits until it is time to speak (Ecclesiastes 3:7).

Job's Opening Analysis of His Suffering

Job is devastated by his experience. He grieves over his losses. It seems it would have been better if he had never been born. Job, like many people in Scripture, is not afraid to express his sorrow, confusion, and hurt. To reinforce his point, the literary form of the book changes from prose to poetry.

Job's Three Friends: Their Arguments

Eliphaz, the most considerate of Job's friends, speaks from the perspective of personal observation. His argument may be summarized as, "If you sin, you suffer." In 4:8, he insists, *As I have seen, those who plow iniquity and sow trouble reap the same."* This sentiment is not entirely wrong, but it goes awry when Eliphaz makes it universal. Scripture admits that sometimes wicked people get away with sin—at least for a time (Psalm 73:3-14). We also know that sometimes God permits the innocent to perish and the upright to be destroyed.

Think about friends who give advice when we face difficult situations. We should be careful about following all their suggestions; bad advice can sometimes sound so good! Even sympathy can be deceptive. The sharpest rebuke Jesus ever gave a disciple was when Peter said that surely Jesus would not have to suffer and be killed (Matthew 16:21-22). Jesus responded, *"Get behind me, Satan! You are a hindrance to me. For you are not setting your mind on the things of God, but on the things of man"* (16:23). Jesus knew he was walking into the painful climax of His earthly ministry, and understood that Satan would want to introduce doubt, self-pity, or any other emotion that would discourage Him. We, too, should weigh the input we receive. While we can appreciate any encouragement and comfort, we should be aware that others' misperceptions or wrong viewpoints may make us question God's care for us, His plans for us, or His heart toward us. We are also especially vulnerable to error in times of great pain. Ask God, and a trusted mentor, to help you discern the truth.

Bildad assumes the stance of the historian, with a strong measure of legal scholarship thrown in. His basic argument is, "You must be sinning, Job." He insists that the wise men of the past will vindicate this assertion: *"Inquire, please, of bygone ages, and consider what the fathers have searched out. … Will they not teach you and tell you and utter words out of their understanding?"* (8:8-10). He is more arrogant and argumentative than Eliphaz. He insists on truth, and he applies it in a particularly painful way: *"If your children have sinned against Him, He has delivered them into the hand of their transgression"* (8:4). Bildad conceives of God as a stern judge who has little patience with frail and sinning humanity.

In his response, Job suggests that he is fighting a losing battle. Who can argue with God? What courtroom would allow Job and God to be placed on an equal footing? *"He is not a man, as I am, that I might answer Him, that we should come to trial together"* (9:32). He accuses God of treating him unfairly by not even specifying a list of charges against him.

Zophar is a dogmatist. He is coarse and blunt in his assertions and bases them on mere assumptions. By the third round of debates, he drops out of the dialogue entirely. He implies that Job is deceitful and is getting what he deserves: *"[God] knows worthless men; when He sees iniquity, will He not consider it?"* (11:11). Zophar regards Job as dense: *"A stupid man will get understanding when a wild donkey's colt is born a man!"* (11:12).

In his reply, Job asserts two complaints. First, God gives no indication He even hears Job's prayers: *"Behold, I cry out, 'Violence!' but I am not answered; I call for help, but there is no justice"* (19:7). Second, God is apparently punishing him even though he is innocent: *"He crushes me with a tempest and multiplies my wounds without cause"* (9:17; see also 7:20). Job ends the second cycle of debate by again defending his innocence: *"For I know that my Redeemer lives, and at the last He will stand upon the earth. And after my skin has been thus destroyed, yet in my flesh I shall see God, whom I shall see for myself, and my eyes shall behold, and not another"* (19:25-27).

Interpreters have differed as to whether Job expected to be redeemed and given life at the end of history. The language he uses certainly allows for that, but this is probably not what Job meant. The word translated *Redeemer* might better be rendered *Vindicator*. Job's immediate concern is his friends' criticism. He is probably thinking more of vindication than of eternal salvation. If he can't have it in this life, he says, he expects it in the future. God Himself, Job's Vindicator, will exonerate him of his friends' foul accusations.

Personalize this lesson.

☑ Job wanted to defend himself before God, but realized that *"[God] is not a man, as I am, that I might answer Him, that we should come to trial together. There is no arbiter between us, who might lay his hand on us both. Let Him take His rod away from me, and let not dread of Him terrify me. Then I would speak without fear of Him, for I am not so in myself"* (Job 9:32-35). This dilemma was resolved with the appearance on earth of the God-man, Jesus Christ, who became the arbitrator between man and God, and who "removed God's rod" from us by taking the punishment for our sins on Himself. *"My little children, I am writing these things to you so that you may not sin. But if anyone does sin, we have an advocate with the Father, Jesus Christ the righteous"* (1 John 2:1).

The amazing thing is that Job foreshadows this eternal Advocate between God and man: *"I know that my Redeemer lives, and at the last He will stand upon the earth. … My eyes shall behold. … My heart faints within me!"* (Job 19:25, 27). Hundreds of years later Jesus walked on the earth and, through His sacrificial death, opened the way for all people to experience God's love. If you have not already accepted His gift of salvation, let Him be your personal Redeemer today. If you have accepted that gift, ask Him to give you a fresh vision of Him that allows you to see Him in all His glory.

Lesson 4

Will the Real God Please Stand Up?
Job 27–37

Memorize God's Word: Job 28:28.

❖ Job 27–28—Job Refutes His Friends' Arguments

1. What is Job's final answer to his friends' accusations (27:1-6)?

   _____

   _____

2. What is the source of wisdom, and how can it be acquired?

   a. Job 28:20-28 _____

   _____

   b. Colossians 2:2-4_____

   _____

   c. James 1:5_____

❖ Job 29–31—Job Evaluates His Life

3. In Job 29–30, Job compares his life in the past with his life in the present. What contrasts does he draw in the following areas?

	Past	Present
Relationship with God	29:2-6	30:11, 18-23

	Past	Present
Standing in the Community	29:7-15, 21-25	20:1-14
Physical and Emotional State	29:18-20	30:15-17, 24-31

4. How does Job assess his standing before God in the following areas?

a. His moral life (Job 31:1-4, 9-12) _____

_____

_____

b. His work life (Job 31:5-8, 13-15) _____

_____

_____

c. His community life (Job 31:16-23) _____

_____

_____

d. His financial life (Job 31:24-25) _____

_____

_____

e. His spiritual life (Job 31:26-28) _____

_____

_____

❖ Job 32–33—A Young Man Named Elihu

5. Why does Elihu feel that he has to speak, and why has he waited so long (32:1-12, 17-20)?

_____

_____

_____

6. Which of Job's claims does Elihu intend to prove false (33:8-10)?

_____

_____

7. Elihu mentions three ways that God speaks to people (33:13-19). What are they?

_____

_____

_____

8. Which of these have you experienced?

_____

_____

_____

9. Can you think of other ways God speaks to us today?

_____

_____

_____

10. Has God ever used suffering to speak to you?

_____

_____

_____

❖ Job 34–37—Establishing a Right View of God

11. In his suffering, and in response to the bad counsel of his friends, what conclusions has Job drawn about God (34:5-9)?

_____

_____

12. What argument does Elihu use to refute these conclusions (34:10-12)?

_____

_____

13. How does Elihu summarize his view of God (37:23-24)?

_____

_____

14. What evidence do we have that God is with us in adversity even though we may not be able to discern His presence?

   a. Deuteronomy 31:6 _____

   _____

   b. Romans 8:35-39_____

   _____

Apply what you have learned. Although many surrounding cultures worshiped nature, Job states that he has been careful not to dishonor God that way: "[If] *my heart has been secretly enticed, and my mouth has kissed my hand, this also would be an iniquity ... for I would have been false to God above*" (Job 31:27-28). Beauty is part of God's plan for the world. He does not, however, want us to worship His lovely creation. The beauty we see in the world is merely an expression of His beauty. Let the world inspire you, but reserve your worship for our beautiful Savior. When you are moved by God's beauty, tell Him how it affects you and how much you enjoy what He has made. Let Him share His pleasure in His creation with you as well.?

Lesson 4 Commentary

Will the Real God Please Stand Up?
Job 27–37

After Job's three friends have exhausted their arguments, Job brings the discussion to a conclusion. He maintains they have not established their claim that he is harboring secret sins. He persists in claiming his innocence and integrity. At the conclusion of his five chapters, Elihu speaks.

Job's Final Self-Justification

Job says his hands are clean and he has done nothing wrong. He gives his understanding of how God deals with the wicked. He agrees that all the terrors one might expect will indeed overcome the wicked, but he differs with his three friends about how quickly disaster overtakes evildoers.

Job acknowledges that God is wise, and our ability to discern that wisdom is deficient. His friends had claimed to see God's plan in what happened to Job. Job shows how silly their thoughts are. He draws a comparison between people's ability to discover gemstones and their inability to mine the depths of God's wisdom, which is far more valuable.

Think about how fervently prospectors searched for riches in the American West. Job 28 describes this obsessive drive to possess gold, silver, and precious gems, then compares it to the search for wisdom; people who want to be wise must search diligently. God is the source of all wisdom, Job says. When the Creator established the ways that everything in the universe would function, *"He said to man, 'Behold, the fear of the Lord, that is wisdom, and to turn away from evil is understanding'"* (28:28).

Job contrasts his present horrible circumstances with how God had blessed him in the past. He had enjoyed the sweet fellowship of his children and God's intimate, daily friendship. He had the community's complete respect. He served others. How things have changed! God now treats him like trash blown about by the wind. And for what crimes has God imposed such a fate? There are none.

Eliphaz had implied Job thought far too much of his wealth, but Job denies that he took pride in possessions. Nor did he turn to false gods. Job denies delighting in his enemies' downfall. His friends claimed Job harbored secret iniquities, but Job denies this as well. He summarizes his anguish by longing for someone to judge his situation impartially: *"Oh, that I had one to hear me! (Here is my signature! Let the Almighty answer me!) Oh, that I had the indictment written by my adversary!"* (31:35). Job says he is willing to live with the consequences of his wrongdoings—if he has any.

Elihu's Rebukes

As Job's self-justification ends, a new voice enters the discussion. Elihu has been observing silently, knowing he is younger than the rest. After hearing all that Job and his friends have to say, he can endure the silence no longer. Job's insistence on justifying himself disturbs Elihu, but the three friends equally bother him. They condemn Job severely, yet cannot make their charges stick. Elihu turns the argument around, asserting that Job is sinning because of his suffering. The sin in question? Prideful self-justification. Job should give God the benefit of the doubt and instead doubt himself. Job says God ignores him and does not respond to his appeals. Elihu claims that God has, in fact, spoken to Job as He has spoken to other people: through dreams and through suffering itself.

Think about how isolated we can feel when we endure pain. We can feel detached from even our closest friends. Worse, our prayers and conversations with God may fall flat. At these times we can draw on our experiences of how God proved His love for us in the past. If you have kept a journal of your relationship with God, now is the time to read it. If God has given you faith to walk with Him through previous obstacles, now is the time to apply faith again: *"Recall the former days when, after you were enlightened, you endured a hard struggle with sufferings"* (Hebrews 10:32). If songs or Scripture verses have lifted your heart in the past, return to them. God wants us to remember how real He was to us before and know that He is the same caring God today, even if He seems hidden.

Elihu invites Job to refute him—if he can: *"But now, hear my speech, O Job, and listen to all my words. ... The Spirit of God has made me, and the breath of the Almighty gives me life. Answer me, if you can; set your words in order before me; take your stand"* (33:1-5). These words assume more weight when we realize that Job does not respond to Elihu's charges. Job may very well feel unable to defend himself against assertions that he knows hold merit.

Elihu chronicles Job's charges against God. Job has charged God with misconduct, and he should not do so. God permits suffering in order to do something in the sufferer: *"God does all these things, twice, three times, with a man, to bring back his soul from the pit, that he may be lighted with the light of life"* (33:29-30). Elihu says the burden of proof is on Job. God should not have to convince Job that He has acted righteously. That should be assumed: *"Will He then make repayment to suit you, because you reject it? For you must choose, and not I; therefore declare what you know"* (34:33).

Elihu argues that God's silence when disaster comes is related to improper human attitudes. People often appeal to God in less than sincere ways. They cry out for vindication, but with an arrogant frame of reference: *"There they cry out, but He does not answer, because of the pride of evil men. Surely God does not hear an empty cry, nor does the Almighty regard it. How much less when you say that you do not see Him, that the case is before Him, and you are waiting for Him!"* (35:12-14). Elihu emphasizes God's purpose in suffering; that is, God desires that His creatures lay aside their pride.

Personalize this lesson.

It's normal to want to avoid difficult life circumstances and wish to be relieved of our sufferings. Our pain can blind us to anything else. But when we press in to God during trials, we can find surprising growth and new perspectives. Job was so hurt and confused by injustice that he was unable to see that God was communicating some important life truths. Elihu is the one who saw this and pointed it out to Job. Elihu said that God wants to *"turn man aside from his deed and conceal pride from a man; He keeps back his soul from the pit"* (33:17-18). God may nudge us along or allow us to experience the refining fire, but He doesn't want us to disconnect from Him or stay as we are. He wants us to grow in relationship with Him and in maturity in Christ. When you're in difficulty, go to God, as Job did. Ask Him what He has for you, what He wants to provide for you, and how He wants to help you grow up in Him.

What Happens When God Shows Up
Job 38:1-40:5

❖ Job 38:1-3—Job Gets His Wish

1. What did Job ask for in Job 31:35 that is granted in Job 38:1?

   _____

   _____

2. How does God demonstrate His presence in each of the following Scriptures, and what does the nature of each of these encounters suggest about Him?

   a. Joshua 5:13-15 _____

   _____

   b. Isaiah 6:1-4_____

   _____

   c. Daniel 3:19-25 _____

   _____

   _____

❖ Job 38:4-15—God the Creator

3. Job called for God to meet him in court (13:20-22), but it is Job, not God, who has been summoned to the witness stand. What subject matter does God quiz Job about in this passage?

   _____

   _____

4. What do these questions reveal about God?

    _____

    _____

5. What do you think God's purpose is in questioning Job?

    _____

    _____

6. How does 1 Peter 1:6-7 describe God's work in the lives of men and women?

    _____

    _____

7. God uses all kinds of circumstances to work in our lives. What has God brought into your life to refine your faith, grow your character, or draw you closer to Him?

    _____

    _____

    _____

❖ Job 38:16-38—God the Designer

8. What building blocks of the universe does God question Job about next?

    _____

    _____

9. What realities is He proving to Job?

    _____

    _____

10. What does God's question in 38:36 imply about His involvement in scientific research and understanding?

    _____

    _____

11. How does 38:36 refute the view that science, by its very nature, conflicts with theology?

_____

_____

❖ Job 38:39–39:30—God the Provider

12. In this passage, God expands the subject matter of Job's examination, moving from geophysics and astronomy to zoology. What animals does God question Job about?

_____

_____

13. What does His involvement with these animals reveal about who He is?

_____

_____

14. How would you relate the implications of God's questions in these verses to Jesus' teaching in Matthew 6:25-33?

_____

_____

_____

15. How does your answer to question 14 apply to your personal circumstances and challenges?

_____

_____

_____

❖ Job 40:1-5—God the Challenger

16. How do you think Job feels now about the charges he made against God in 10:8-9 and 23:3-7?

_____

_____

17. Have you ever felt that God was treating you unfairly? What is the right perspective on God, regardless of the circumstances?

_____

_____

_____

_____

18. Consider the vast number of scientific discoveries that have been made in the thousands of years since Job's day. If God asked these same questions today, would there be anyone qualified to answer them? Why or why not?

_____

_____

_____

_____

Apply what you have learned. When God paused after His first round of questions and commanded Job to answer Him, all Job could say was, *"I am of small account; what shall I answer you? ... I will not answer"* (40:4-5). And he put his hand over his mouth. He had spoken brash words, and he was silenced. Thankfully, we have a gracious God who allows His children to speak to Him openly and frankly. John says, *"We have come to know and to believe the love that God has for us. God is love"* (1 John 4:16). Because God is love, He is patient and kind with us (1 Corinthians 13:4). Still, we should have the attitude of David: *"Let the words of my mouth and the meditation of my heart be acceptable in Your sight, O Lord, my Rock and my Redeemer"* (Psalm 19:14). We can speak freely, knowing we are loved, and yet still voice our thoughts with respect.

What Happens When God Shows Up
Job 38:1-40:5

Job wants God to hear his complaint. In chapters 38 and 39, God appears, but not to listen to Job. Instead, He challenges Job with questions about the universe. Job finds that he, rather than God, must give an account.

God appears to Job *"out of the whirlwind"* (38:1), suggesting His holiness—and His displeasure. He says Job has obscured the truth and spoken about things he knew nothing about. Instead of answering questions, God asks them. His first question contains a rebuke: *"Who is this that darkens counsel by words without knowledge?"* (38:2). Job has not made others wiser; Job has darkened the minds.

Job needs to prepare himself for a flood of questions: *"Dress for action like a man; I will question you, and you make it known to Me"* (38:3). God will give Job an examination that covers many fields: astronomy, cosmology, meteorology, oceanography, and zoology. In one sense, these questions are rhetorical; they expect no answer. In any case, Job lacks the qualifications to answer any of them, and that is the point.

The first question is typical: *"Where were you when I laid the foundation of the earth? Tell Me, if you have understanding"* (38:4). Job, of course, does not understand. He has, in the heat of his sufferings, forgotten that man must observe the limits the Creator set for him. God, by contrast, knows all there is to know.

God governs matters that creatures take for granted: *"Have you commanded the morning since your days began, and caused the dawn to know its place?"* (38:12). The Creator continues to exercise moment-by-moment control over everything. It should be noted that God does not attribute the dawn to the earth's rotation or describe it as an autonomous process. All present processes, even those described by science as "natural," have their source in

God: *"For by* [Christ] *all things were created, in heaven and on earth, visible and invisible, whether thrones or dominions or rulers or authorities—all things were created through Him and for Him. And He is before all things, and in Him all things hold together"* (Colossians 1:16-17). Jesus determines the orbit of every electron and of every planet: *"He is the radiance of the glory of God and the exact imprint of His nature, and He upholds the universe by the word of His power"* (Hebrews 1:3).

God turns to matters that are remote from human beings. He speaks of the deepest parts of the ocean and of death's gates. He questions Job's knowledge of *"the expanse of the earth"* (Job 38:18). He then questions, in divine irony, *"You know, for you were born then, and the number of your days is great!"* (38:21).

Think about how science can now explain most of these natural processes. Yet it cannot explain how all the functions became coordinated in just the right balance or establish who set all these processes in motion. God, as the Source of all created things, cannot be discovered by the scientific method. NASA astronomer Robert Jastrow, in his book *God and the Astronomers*, says, "For the scientist who has lived by his faith in the power of reason, the story [of where the earth came from] ends like a bad dream. He has scaled the mountains of ignorance; he is about to conquer the highest peak. As he pulls himself over the final rock, he is greeted by a band of theologians who have been sitting there for centuries" (1992, p. 107).

Unlike God, Job cannot limit or direct the stars in their courses. He cannot even describe what takes place there: *"Do you know the ordinances of the heavens? Can you establish their rule on the earth?"* (38:33). God explains that He sends the lightning bolts to their appointed destinations, and it is He who gives people the ability to relate to God: *"Who has put wisdom in the inward parts or given understanding to the mind?"* (38:36).

God shifts His examination to the animal creation, speaking of 10 animals. Some are fierce, others weak; some are shy, others bizarre.

Humans do not closely observe most of their lives. Together they exhibit God's widespread, watchful care over His creation. His first question is intriguing: *"Can you hunt the prey for the lion, or satisfy the appetite of the young lions?"* (38:39). We think lions take care of themselves, but God claims credit for providing food for even the fiercest predators.

God names other creatures, including the ostrich. A mother ostrich seems foolish and treats her young with disdain, yet she can outrun a horse when threatened. Who supplied her with this advantage? Job is at a loss to explain it all, much less to accomplish or duplicate any of these remarkable achievements. At the conclusion of this parade of power and wisdom, God reminds Job where the conversation began: *"Shall a faultfinder contend with the Almighty? He who argues with God, let him answer it"* (40:2).

Think about how the great majority of plants and animals live and die outside of human contact or observation. Although mankind is largely unaware of the lives of these flora and fauna, this passage shows that God watches over every living thing—and takes great delight in them.

It is mankind's privilege and responsibility to care for the world. At Creation, "God blessed [Adam and Eve]. And God said to them, 'Be fruitful and multiply and fill the earth and subdue it, and have dominion over the fish of the sea and over the birds of the heavens and over every living thing that moves on the earth'" (Genesis 1:28). As stewards or caretakers of what God designed, we should not misuse or squander its resources but wisely manage and protect them.

After hearing God's series of unanswerable challenges, Job responds, *"Behold, I am of small account; what shall I answer you? I lay my hand on my mouth. I have spoken once, and I will not answer; twice, but I will proceed no further"* (Job 40:4-5). Job knows when he is defeated. He sees his weakness, and (more importantly) his limits.

Personalize this lesson.

☑ As God questions Job, nothing He says answers Job's questions of "Why? What did I do?" The issue of whether Job is guilty or innocent is off the table. Instead, God speaks from a vastly different perspective: namely, who He is. God's sovereignty is immense, and no corner of the universe escapes His attention and care. While this doesn't answer Job's questions, it does ground him again in God's reality. He sees himself and God clearly, and that is enough. When you are in a place of suffering, ask God to reveal His character to you again, and to give you a fresh view of both His immense sovereignty and His close, personal attention.

Job Learns the Truth About God
Job 40:6-42:17

❖ Job 40:6-14—God Challenges Job

1. What did Job confess in 40:1-4?

   _____

   _____

2. What brought him to this conclusion?

   _____

   _____

3. What issue does God bring up in Job 40:8?

   _____

4. In reality, what had Job been doing when he accused God of being unfair?

   _____

   _____

5. In verses 9-14, which of His attributes and abilities does God challenge Job to equal?

   _____

   _____

6. To what conclusion is God leading Job with this challenge?

   _____

   _____

❖ Job 40:15–41:34—God Teaches Job

7.　What two creatures does God use as illustrations in His second rebuke of Job?

_____

_____

8.　What might God's purpose be in focusing Job's attention on these creatures?

_____

_____

9.　How does God personalize this lesson for Job in 41:10-11?

_____

_____

10.　What similar principles does Paul state in Romans 9:20-21 and 11:33-36?

_____

_____

11.　How might these principles impact your view of your current circumstances?

_____

_____

_____

❖ Job 42:1-6—God Humbles Job

12.　What conclusion about God does Job voice in these verses?

_____

_____

13.　What led him to this conclusion?

_____

_____

14. Job quotes God twice in 42:2-6. What does he recall, and how does he respond to what God said?

_____

_____

15. How has Job's attitude toward God been changed by this personal encounter with Him?

_____

_____

❖ Job 42:7-9—God Rebukes Job's Friends

16. Why is God angry with Job's friends?

_____

_____

17. Why is it so important that we represent God accurately when we tell others about Him?

_____

_____

_____

18. What can we do to be sure that what we say about God is true?

_____

_____

_____

19. What does God require Job's friends to do to be reconciled to Him and restored to friendship with Job?

_____

_____

20. How does God refer to Job in His instructions to Job's friends?

_____

_____

❖ Job 42:10-17—God Restores Job's Blessings

21. What does God do to restore Job's position in his family and community (verses 10-11)?

_____

_____

22. Do you think God ever explained to Job why he had suffered? Why or why not?

_____

_____

23. How will what you've learned from Job help you when you face unexplained suffering?

_____

_____

Apply what you have learned. When Job's friends offended God by the errors they passed along as truth and by the way they mistreated Job, God required sacrifices to atone for their sin and reestablish peace with Him. He went even further and had them ask Job to pray for them, which meant they also had to ask Job's forgiveness. This illustrates the importance God places on restoring relationships after a divisive or hurtful confrontation. Second Corinthians 5:18 says that God first *"through Christ reconciled us to Himself"* then *"gave us the ministry of reconciliation."* God does not want our sins to create barriers between us and others. When we repair a relationship after a breach, blessings can flow freely among us. Ask God to reveal to you if there is an unrepaired relationship in your life. What would He have you do with it? What about the relationship might be out of your control? What reassurance or comfort might God have for you in this case?

Job Learns the Truth About God
Job 40:6–42:17

God's first rebuke challenged Job's right to accuse God of injustice. In God's second rebuke, He asks Job to consider the *behemoth* and *leviathan*. Job is then to ponder his place in the created order and the suitability of calling God's justice into question. Job makes a humble confession of weakness and repents of his pride. God then restores Job and rebukes his mistaken friends.

Think about what Satan does at this point in the narrative. Although he never appears again, he is probably in the wings, watching. He has lost the challenge. Job's faith was strong enough to hold out against his attacks. He will continue his subversive attacks on other souls, and still continues today. Paul warned the Corinthians not to *"be outwitted by Satan; for we are not ignorant of his designs"* (2 Corinthians 2:11).

God's Second Rebuke

God reminds Job that only He can adorn Himself with glory, splendor, honor and majesty. God will not submit to Job's questioning unless he can show the same power, including the power to end the lives of the human race and put them in the grave.

Two more examples from nature illustrate God's greatness. The first is the frightening *behemoth*. This animal's identity is unclear. Whatever he was, he was no match for God. God also describes an even more impressive creature called *leviathan* that was found on the high seas. No living animal matches the description, so it is likely that leviathan is extinct today.

God's point is clear and unmistakable: *"No one is so fierce that he dares to stir* [leviathan] *up. Who then is he who can stand before Me?"* (41:10). God is the uncreated Source of all things and answerable to no one.

Think about circumstances that are out of our control. We cannot control ferocious animals, weather, rulers, or death. We cannot exert our wills and make the world serve our purposes. Nevertheless, pride raises its ugly head in every realm of life, beginning as far back as Genesis 11:4, when the people of Babel said, *"Come, let us build ourselves a city and a tower with its top in the heavens, and let us make a name for ourselves."* They didn't need God, and they thought their tower would prove their greatness.

People can live their entire lives without acknowledging that there is a Supreme Being to whom they owe everything: *"In the pride of his face the wicked does not seek Him; all his thoughts are, 'There is no God'"* (Psalm 10:4). It is mercy when God confronts us with our pride, as He did Job, and we acknowledge that *"salvation and glory and power belong to our God"* (Revelation 19:1), and not to ourselves.

Job's Confession

Job's trials were part of a larger picture, which he and his friends cannot see. Job still doesn't know why he suffered; however, he does know God much more deeply. Job summarizes what he has learned: Before suffering, he thought God was in some way limited, and that his personal goodness must be taken into account. Now, he knows better: *"I know that You can do all things, and that no purpose of Yours can be thwarted"* (42:2). Job's protests were based on ignorance: *"I have uttered what I did not understand, things too wonderful for me, which I did not know"* (42:3). Part of wisdom lies in discerning what we don't know. All believers, at some point, must place their hands over their mouths and simply keep quiet.

Now that Job has encountered God directly, he has come to a different conclusion: *"I had heard of You by the hearing of the ear, but now my eye*

sees You; therefore I despise myself, and repent in dust and ashes" (42:5-6).
Instead of diminishing Job, this experience improved him.

God's Deliverance of Job

Following the questioning, God again extends His kindness to Job. In the
words of James, *"You have heard of the steadfastness of Job, and you have seen
the purpose of the Lord, how the Lord is compassionate and merciful"* (5:11).
God's mercy begins by vindicating Job before his friends: *"The Lord said
to Eliphaz the Temanite: 'My anger burns against you and against your two
friends, for you have not spoken of Me what is right, as my servant Job has"*
(Job 42:7). God commands the three men to offer burnt offerings to atone
for their pride and doctrinal ignorance. Their restoration to fellowship with
God, however, depends on Job: *"My servant Job shall pray for you, for I will
accept his prayer not to deal with you according to your folly. For you have not
spoken of Me what is right, as my servant Job has"* (42:8). All opinions are
not equally valid, and God takes a dim view of people such as Job's friends,
who might have destroyed Job had he accepted their views.

Following Job's prayer, God not only restores Job's original wealth, He
doubles Job's property. His brothers and sisters (unmentioned before
this) come to see him and his old friends return. In fact, they add to his
prosperity by contributing money and jewelry. Additionally, Job begins a
new family, again producing seven sons and three daughters.

Think about the spiritual issues that Job may
never have to wrestle with again. He had assurance
that God loved him, and he was less likely to feel
"separation anxiety" when God seemed distant. A
time of blessing and peace had replaced the agonizing tests.
He was probably more sensitive and generous in the way he
reached out to hurting people. What other ways do you
think he changed? Perhaps we can learn from his experience
after having endured this journey with him.

Job had thought that his brow was buried forever in the dust (16:15), but
God has proved him wrong. He would, in fact, live to an exceptional age,
find joy in his great-grandchildren, and become a man of enduring fame.

Personalize this lesson.

☑ The greatest theme of this book is the character of God. We have learned a lot about Him through the different opinions expressed and the final revelations from God Himself. The three friends were lopsided in their theology. Pastor and author Ray Stedman said that they "meant to uphold God's righteousness, but they said nothing about His mercy, His compassion, His patience, His willingness to reach out and wait for men and give them opportunity to repent." Their actions reflected their beliefs—they never offered to pray for Job or asked how they could help relieve his suffering; they just probed to find Job's sins so they could correct him. It's not unusual for people to lean too far the other way, either—being so generous and forgiving that they fail to confront sin.

God, however, knew Job well enough that He trusted in Job's steadfast heart toward Him. Job suffered greatly under Satan's attacks—so greatly that he wished he had never been born. He questioned God, lamented, and grieved. Yet God still said to Eliphaz, *"You have not spoken of me what is right, as Job has"* (42:7). Job never did come to know the answer to his questions, yet he did come to know God.

What questions has Job's experience caused you to ask God? How can you continue in steadfastness even though you have these questions? Ask God to help you experience Him and encounter His truth personally so that, like Job, you can remain faithful in spite of times of darkness.

Small Group Leader's Guide

While *Engaging God's Word* is great for personal study, it is generally even more effective and enjoyable when studied with others. Studying with others provides different perspectives and insights, care, prayer support, and fellowship that studying on your own does not. Depending on your personal circumstances, consider studying with your family or spouse, with a friend, in a Sunday school, with a small group at church, work, or in your neighborhood, or in a mentoring relationship.

In a traditional Community Bible Study class, your study would involve a proven four-step method: personal study, a small group discussion facilitated by a trained leader, a lecture covering the passage of Scripture, and a written commentary about the same passage. *Engaging God's Word* provides two of these four steps with the study questions and commentary. When you study with a group, you add another of these—the group discussion. And if you enjoy teaching, you could even provide a modified form of the fourth, the lecture, which in a small group setting might be better termed a wrap-up talk.

Here are some suggestions to help leaders facilitate a successful group study.

1. Decide how long you would like each group meeting to last. For a very basic study, without teaching, time for fellowship, or group prayer, plan on one hour. If you want to allow for fellowship before the meeting starts, add at least 15 minutes. If you plan to give a short teaching, add 15 or 20 minutes. If you also want time for group prayer, add another 10 or 15 minutes. Depending on the components you include for your group, each session will generally last between one and two hours.

2. Set a regular time and place to meet. Meeting in a church classroom or a conference room at work is fine. Meeting in a home is also a good option, and sometimes more relaxed and comfortable.

3. Publicize the study and/or personally invite people to join you.

4. Begin praying for those who have committed to come. Continue to pray for them individually throughout the course of the study.

5. Make sure everyone has his or her own book at least a week before you meet for the first time.

6. Encourage group members to read the first lesson and do the questions before they come to the group meeting.

7. Prepare your own lesson.

8. Prepare your wrap-up talk, if you plan to give one. Here is a simple process for developing a wrap-up talk:

   a. Divide the passage you are studying into two or three divisions. Jot down the verses for each division and describe the content of each with one complete sentence that answers the question, "What is the passage about?"

   b. Decide on the central idea of your wrap-up talk. The central idea is the life-changing principle found in the passage that you believe God wants to implant in the hearts and minds of your group. The central idea answers the question, "What does God want us to learn from this passage?"

   c. Provide one illustration that would make your central idea clear and meaningful to your group. This could be an illustration from your own life, or a story you've read or heard somewhere else.

   d. Suggest one application that would help your group put the central idea into practice.

   e. Choose an aim for your wrap-up talk. The aim answers the question, "What does God want us to do about it?" It encourages specific change in your group's lives, if they choose to respond to the central idea of the passage. Often it takes the form of a question you will ask your group: "Will you, will I choose to … ?"

9. Show up early to the study so you can arrange the room, set up the refreshments (if you are serving any), and welcome people as they arrive.

10. Whether your meeting includes a fellowship time or not, begin the discussion time promptly each week. People appreciate it when you respect their time. Transition into the discussion with prayer, inviting God to guide the discussion time and minister personally to each person present.

11. Model enthusiasm to the group. Let them know how excited you are about what you are learning—and your eagerness to hear what God is teaching them.

12. As you lead through the questions, encourage everyone to participate, but don't force anyone. If one or two people tend to dominate the discussion, encourage quieter ones to participate by saying something like, "Let's hear from someone who hasn't shared yet." Resist the urge to teach during discussion time. This time is for your group to share what they have been discovering.

13. Try to allow time after the questions have been discussed to talk about the "Apply what you have learned," "Think about" and "Personalize this lesson" sections. Encourage your group members in their efforts to partner with God in allowing Him to transform their lives.

14. Transition into the wrap-up talk, if you are doing one (see number 8).

15. Close in prayer. If you have structured your group to allow time for prayer, invite group members to pray for themselves and one another, especially focusing on the areas of growth they would like to see in their lives as a result of their study. If you have not allowed time for group prayer, you as leader can close this time.

16. Before your group finishes their final lesson, start praying and planning for what your next *Engaging God's Word* study will be.

About Community Bible Study

For almost 40 years Community Bible Study
has taught the Word of God through in-depth,
community-based Bible studies. With nearly 700
classes in the United States as well as classes in
more than 70 countries, Community Bible Study purposes to be an
"every-person's Bible study, available to all."

Classes for men, women, youth, children, and even babies, are all
designed to make members feel loved, cared for, and accepted—
regardless of age, ethnicity, socio-economic status, education, or
church membership. Because Bible study is most effective in one's heart
language, Community Bible Study curriculum has been translated into
more than 50 languages.

Community Bible Study makes every effort to stand in the center of the
mainstream of historic Christianity, concentrating on the essentials of
the Christian faith rather than denominational distinctives. Community
Bible Study respects different theological views, preferring to focus on
helping people to know God through His Word, grow deeper in their
relationships with Jesus, and be transformed into His likeness.

Community Bible Study's focus ... is to glorify God by providing
in-depth Bible studies and curriculum in a Christ-centered, grace-filled,
and philosophically safe environment.

Community Bible Study's passion ... is the transformation of
individuals, families, communities, and generations through the power
of God's Word, making disciples of the Lord Jesus Christ.

Community Bible Study's relationship with local churches ... is one
of support and respect. Community Bible Study classes are composed of
people from many different churches; they are designed to complement
and not compete with the ministry of the local church. Recognizing that
the Lord has chosen the local church as His primary channel of ministry,
Community Bible Study encourages class members to belong to and
actively support their local churches and to be servants and leaders in
their congregations.

Do you want to experience lasting transformation in your life? Are you ready to go deeper in God's Word? There is probably a Community Bible Study near you! Find out by visiting www.findmyclass.org or scan the QR code on this page.

For more information:

Call   800-826-4181

Email   info@communitybiblestudy.org

Web   www.communitybiblestudy.org

Class   www.findmyclass.org

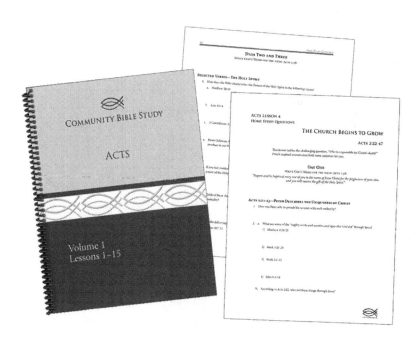

Where will your next Bible study adventure take you?

Engage Bible Studies help you discover the joy and the richness of God's Word and apply it your life.

Check out these titles for your next adventure:

Engaging God's Word: Genesis

Engaging God's Word: Daniel

Engaging God's Word: Mark

Engaging God's Word: Luke

Engaging God's Word: Galatians

Engaging God's Word: Ephesians

Engaging God's Word: Philippians

Engaging God's Word: Colossians

Engaging God's Word: Hebrews

Engaging God's Word: 1 & 2 Peter

Engaging God's Word: James

Engaging God's Word: Revelation

New adventures available soon:

Engaging God's Word: Deuteronomy

Engaging God's Word: Ruth & Esther

Engaging God's Word: Acts

Engaging God's Word: 1 & 2 Thessalonians

Also coming soon:

Engage Bible Studies in Spanish!

Available at Amazon.com and in fine bookstores.

Visit engagebiblestudies.com

Made in the USA
San Bernardino, CA
22 September 2016